St. Elizabe

Animal Builders

Written by Jon Mudge   Illustrated by Bill Pappas

📖 ScottForesman

A Division of HarperCollins*Publishers*

Who builds a house of wax?

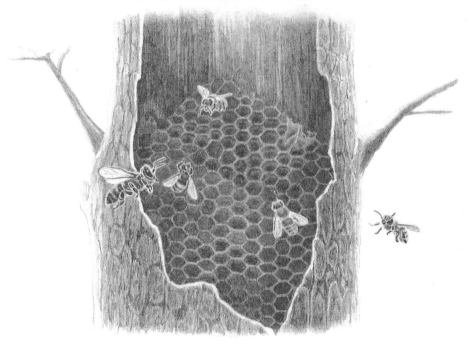

Honey bees do.
They use wax to make honeycombs.
They make rows of little rooms
called cells.

Who builds a house of paper?

Wasps do.
They use paper to make nests.
The queen chews wood to make
the paper.

Who builds a house of clay?

Ovenbirds do.
Ovenbirds use clay to make nests.
Their nests look like little ovens.

4

Who builds a house of leaves?

Tailorbirds do.
They use leaves to make nests. They
sew leaves together with spider silk.

Who builds a house of wood?

Beavers do.
Beavers use big and small branches
to make dams. They use mud and
stones to keep the sticks together.

Who builds an underground
neighborhood?

Prairie dogs do.
They use their noses and paws to dig
tunnels. They make streets to run on
and houses to live in.

Who builds amazing houses?

These animals do!